T0194323

Life

Life

*Light and Dark,
Joy and Anguish*

Sister Mary Faith

iUniverse®

LIFE
LIGHT AND DARK, JOY AND ANGUISH

Scripture quotations marked KJV are from the Holy Bible, King James Version (Authorized Version). First published in 1611. Quoted from the KJV Classic Reference Bible, Copyright © 1983 by The Zondervan Corporation

iUniverse books may be ordered through booksellers or by contacting:

iUniverse
1663 Liberty Drive
Bloomington, IN 47403
www.iuniverse.com
844-349-9409

ISBN: 978-1-6632-0479-0 (sc)
ISBN: 978-1-6632-0481-3 (hc)
ISBN: 978-1-6632-0480-6 (e)

Library of Congress Control Number: 2020913883

Print information available on the last page.

iUniverse rev. date: 10/08/2020

To write this book, at night before going to sleep, I asked the Lord to inspire me. If I had an inspiration, I typed it into my computer. Thank You so very much, my dear friend Jesus, for helping me find the right words.

AND FROM THE DARKNESS CAME A GREAT LIGHT!

Biblical References to Light and Dark in Holy Scripture

And God said, "Let
There be light."

God saw that the light
Was good,
And He
Separated the light
From the darkness

God called the light
Day, and the darkness
He called night.
And there was evening, and
There was morning,
The first day. (Genesis 1:3–5)

That day—may it turn
To darkness; may God
Not care about it; may
No light shine on it. (Job 3:4)

He reveals the deep
Things of darkness and
Brings utter darkness
Into the light

They grope in darkness
With no light;
He makes them
Stagger like drunkards. (Job 12:22, 25)

He despairs of escaping
The realm of darkness; he is
Marked for the sword. (Job 15:22)

My days have passed, my
Plans are shattered.
Yet the desires of my heart
Turn night into day; in the face of
Darkness, light is near. (Job 17:11–12)

What you decide on will
Be done, and light will shine
On your ways. (Job 17:28)

There are those who are against the light,
Who do not know its ways,
Or stay in its paths

In the dark, thieves
Break into houses, but by
Day they shut themselves
In; they want nothing to do
With the light. For all

Of them, midnight is their
Morning; they make friends
With the terrors of darkness. (Job 24:13, 16–17)

Can His forces be numbered?
On whom does His light not rise? (Job 25:3)

He marks the horizon on
The face of the waters for a
Boundary between light and darkness. (Job 26:10)

When His lamp shone on my
Head, and by His light I walked
Through the darkness! (Job 29)

Yet when I hoped for good,
Evil came; when I looked for
Light, then came darkness. (Job 30:26)

God has delivered me from
Going down to the pit, and I shall
Live to enjoy the light of life

To turn them back from the Pit, that the light of life may shine
On them. (Job 33:28, 30)

Blessed are those who have
Learned to acclaim you, who
Walk in the light of your presence, LORD. (Psalm 89:15)

You have set our iniquities
Before you, our secret sins in
The light of your presence. (Psalm 90:8)

Sister Mary Faith

Light shines on the
Righteous and joy on the
Upright in heart. (Psalm 97:11)

As with a garment; He stretches
Out the heavens like a tent. (Psalm)

Even in darkness light
Dawns for the upright, for
Those who are gracious and
Compassionate and righteous. (Psalm 112:4)

Your word is a lamp
For my feet, a light on my
Path ... The unfolding of your word
Gives light; it gives understanding
To the simple. (Psalm 119:105, 130)

Even the darkness will not
Be dark to you; the night will
Shine like the day, for the
Darkness is as light to you. (Psalm 139:12)

Light in a messenger's
Eyes bring joy to the heart,
And good news gives health
To the bones. (Proverbs 15:30)

I saw that wisdom is better
Than folly, just as light is better
Than darkness. (Ecclesiastes 2:13)

Come, descendants of Jacob, let
Us walk in the light of the Lord. (Isaiah 2)

In that day they will roar
Over it like the roaring of the
Sea. And if one looks over
The land, there is only darkness
And distress; even the sun will
Be darkened by clouds. (Isaiah 5:30)

Nevertheless, there will be gloom for
Those who were in distress. In the past, He
Humbled the land of Zebulun and the land
Of Nephtali, but in the future He will honor
Galilee of the nations, by the Way of the
Sea, beyond the Jordan.

The people walking in darkness have
Seen a great light; on those living in the
Land of deep darkness, a light has dawned. (Isaiah 9:1–2)

The stars of heaven and their
Constellations will not show their light.
The rising sun will be darkened and the
Moon will not give its light. (Isaiah 13:10)

I will lead the blind by ways they have
Not known, along unfamiliar paths I will
Guide them; I will turn the darkness into light
Before them and make rough places
Smooth. These are the things I will do; I will not
Forsake them. (Isaiah 42:16)

He says: It is too small a
Thing for you to be my servant
To restore the tribes of Jacob and
Bring back those of Israel I have
Kept. I will also make you a light
For the Gentiles, that my
Salvation may reach to the ends
Of the earth. (Isaiah 49:6)

Listen to me, my people; hear
Me, my nation; Instruction will go out from me;
My justice will be
A light to the nations. (Isaiah 51:4)

Arise, shine, for your light
Has come, and the glory of the LORD rises upon you …
The sun will no more be
Your light by day, nor will the
Brightness of the moon shine on you, for the LORD will be
Your everlasting light, and
Your God will be your glory.

Your sun will never set
Again, and your moon will wane no more; the LORD
Will be your everlasting
Light, and your days of
Sorrow will end. (Isaiah 60:1, 19–20)

I looked at the earth, and
It was formless and empty;
And at the heavens, and their
Light was gone. (Jeremiah 4:23)

Every good and perfect gift
Is from above, coming down from
The Father of heavenly lights, who
Does not change like shifting
Shadows. (James 1:17)

But you are a chosen people,
A royal priesthood, a holy nation,
God's special possession, that
You may declare the praises of
Him who called you out of
Darkness into His wonderful
Light. (1 Peter 9)

This is a message we have
Heard from Him and declare to
You: God is light; in Him there
Is no darkness at all. (1 John 5)

There will be no more night.
They will not need the light of a
Lamp or the light of the sun, for the
Lord God will give them light.
And they will reign forever and
Ever. (Revelation 22:5)

About noon as I came near
Damascus, suddenly a bright
Light from heaven flashed
Around me.

My companions saw the light,
But they did not understand the
Voice of Him who was speaking to me. (Acts 22:6, 9)

To open their eyes and turn
Them from darkness to light, and
From the power of Satan to God,
So that they may receive
Forgiveness of sins and a place
Among those who are sanctified
By faith in me

That the Messiah would
Suffer and, as the first to rise from
The dead, would bring the message
Of light to His own people and to
The Gentiles. (Acts 26:18, 23)

If you are convinced that you
Are a guide for the blind, a light for
Those who are in the dark. (Romans 2:19)

The night is nearly over; the
Day is almost here. So put away
The deeds of darkness and put
On the armor of light. (Romans 13:12)

The god of this age has blinded
The minds of unbelievers, so they
Cannot see the light of the gospel
That displays the glory of Christ,
Who is the image of God.

For our light and momentary
Troubles are achieving for us an
Eternal glory that far outweighs
Them all. (2 Corinthians 4:4, 17)

For you once were darkness,
But now you are light in the Lord.
Live as children of light (for
The fruit of the light consists in
All goodness, righteousness, and truth).

But everything exposed by
The light becomes visible—and
Everything that is illuminated becomes a light. (Ephesians 5:8, 13)

And giving joyful thanks to the
Father, who has qualified you to
Share in the inheritance of His
Holy people in the kingdom of
Light. (Colossians 1:12)

You are the children of the
Light and the children of the day.
We do not belong to the night or
To the dark. (1 Thessalonians 5:5)

The Annunciation

The Annunciation
(The Announcement)

In the sixth month, the angel Gabriel was
Sent from God to a city of Galilee named
Nazareth, to a virgin betrothed to a man
Whose name was Joseph, of the House of
David. And the virgin's name was Mary.

And the angel said to her, "Do not be
Afraid, Mary, for you have found favor with
God."

And behold, you will conceive a son. You
Shall call His name, Jesus. And Mary said
To the angel, "How will this be, since I am
A virgin?"

And the angel answered her. "The Holy
Spirit will come upon you, and the power
Of the Most High will overshadow you;
Therefore, the child to be born will be
Called Holy—the Son of God." (Luke 1:26–27, 30–31, 34)

I t is easy for me to believe in the Immaculate Conception. Eve and then Adam fell from grace. Their descendants fell as well, except for the Blessed Virgin Mary, the second, Eve, and her Son, the Word incarnate, the second, Adam. Both Mary and Jesus were free from original sin and fallen nature from conception.

Jesus Christ Is True God and True Man

Jesus became a man to redeem humankind from the slavery of sin. If one of His parents were subject to original sin, His human nature would be too. Therefore, the Blessed Virgin Mary was not only born free of original sin, but she was also conceived without the taint of it. Thus, the Holy Child, born of the union of the Holy Spirit and Mary, was able to expiate for the sins of humankind.

The Immaculate Conception of Mary enabled her to be the Mother of God. She is pure in mind, body, and soul of necessity. Her conception points to His. His conception refers to hers.

The Blessed Virgin Mary is the spouse of God, the Mother of God, the sister of God, and the daughter of God. She is not a mother-in-law or an aunt.

Jesus never married. Some believe He did. If He was and is true God and true man, He would know He had to die to deliver humankind. If He knew that, He would not have wanted to leave a widow and children.

Sister Mary Faith

The Blessed Virgin Mary was the Mother of God. She was a child of God. So she was also a daughter of God. Mary understands us. She understands our joys and sorrows because she has lived them.

M y mom is the queen of all the angels and saints. My dad is God of heaven and earth. My brother is Lord of lords and King of kings. My spouse is the one who gives the breath of life to the universe and all its galaxies.

God wrote *the* book on suffering. To understand suffering, we must start before time existed. God the Father spoke a word of love. The word He spoke is God the Son. God the Father and God the Son spoke a word of love. That word is the Holy Spirit. God the Father, Son, and the Holy Spirit have always existed together.

The holy Trinity loved, and the angels were created. The angel most like God was the most enlightened, intelligent, and beautiful of the angels. His very name, Lucifer, meant light and enlightenment.

God loved again. He created Adam and Eve. Out of love, God bestowed two gifts on them. They were able to name and rule over the animals.

The first created being to suffer was Lucifer. He was jealous of Adam and Eve. He was full of pride. He wondered how God dared to give a piece of clay, Adam, and a mere bone, Eve, gifts. After all, he was a pure spirit. He was radiant, brilliant, and beautiful. He had always thanked God for making him so much better than any other created being. God never gave Lucifer any gifts like those He gave Adam and Eve.

He decided to get even with God.

Lucifer convinced some of the other angels to rebel against God. He would rule over heaven instead of God. His jealousy and pride blinded his intellect. He had been given the precious gift of enlightenment. He threw himself into darkness, hell. He failed to realize that a created being could never take the place of one who had always existed.

He was no longer Lucifer. He had become Satan. He was resolute in his vow of revenge. If he could not have heaven, neither would Adam and Eve. He would go after the easiest of the two first—that bone thing, Eve. He would persuade her to turn against God. Then she would persuade Adam to do the same.

As a consequence, suffering and death would enter the beautiful, happy, perfect world God created on earth.

God never wanted anyone to suffer. Only someone perfect and unblemished could regain heaven for humankind. God loved again. Jesus was born. God could not be more vulnerable.

Jesus took the form of a slave to redeem humankind. He agonized over His suffering. He obeyed His Father. Christ was a suffering servant.

Mary followed in her child's footsteps. He knew sorrow. She became Our Lady of Sorrows.

The promise of heaven was restored to humankind. The King of Kings and His queen, our Lady, Queen of the Angels and Saints, reigns forever. Alleluia!

Mary experienced light and dark, agony and ecstasy, at the presentation of her firstborn son. She was told He would be the ruler of nations, and a sword of sorrow would pierce her heart.

During the recitation of the rosary, I thought about the finding in the temple. Jesus became obedient to His parents. The great I Am, the pure, white light of God followed the Ten Commandments He had established. He honored His father and mother. His obedience to them in the temple foreshadowed His obedience to death on a cross.

The Agony in the Garden

"I Am."

Jesus was afraid but resolute.

To protect their lives and the life of the temple in Jerusalem, the Pharisees and the Sadducees had to stop the threat to both—Jesus. With the death of Jesus, the leading Jewish men at the time felt that they had achieved their goal. The physical temple in Jerusalem fell in AD 70. However, Jesus was the embodiment of the temple.

The way of life the Pharisees and Sadducees wanted to continue ended with the end of the life of Jesus. When Christ said, "It is consummated," the embodiment of the true temple fell. A new temple was raised from the ashes of the old one. It is the temple of the way of eternity, the truth of love, and the life of service to others regardless of the cost.

Sister Mary Faith

Mary accepted His death.

Jesus Christ ascends to heaven.

Sister Mary Faith

All things will work toward the good for those who love God. That good is an eternity spent in love and joy with God, our Lady, the angels, and the saints.

Sister Mary Faith

Love loosens; it does not hold tight.

Sister Mary Faith

Love never grows old.

When we are cross with others, we give them a cross to carry.

My poor God! What have I done to you?

Forgive me, for I know not what I am doing. Truly this is the Son of God.

Sister Mary Faith

In Matthew 14:13–21, Jesus uses His sense of humor to teach His disciples. Jesus tells them to feed the crowd. His disciples were as poor as church mice. They must have wondered at His commandment to feed everyone in such a lonely place. Perhaps they thought He had been out in the Palestine sun too long.

He baited them. I envision Him telling the disciples to see how far the five loaves would go after the blessing. They might have looked at Him incredulously after the crowds had been fed; there was more left than what they had started with.

I see Jesus standing, laughing with His head thrown back and His hands on His hips. They trusted Him. What was needed had been provided.

The Lord taught when He took a stroll on the deep water. Peter wanted nothing more than to go out to Him; he put one leg over the side of the boat and then the other leg, got his balance, and started walking toward Jesus.

Then fear crept in. His hope left him, and he started to sink. Jesus reached down and gave him a hand up. Perhaps Jesus laughed gently as He said, "Come on, Peter, let's get you out of there. Trust me."

Peter was cold and wet but gratefully alive.

We are in good hands when we go out too far and start to go under. The Lord is always ready to extend a hand to save us from the murky waters of sin. All we have to do is grasp His hand; He will do the rest.

M ama, Papa, Jesu Christe, et Spiritu Sanctu, please forgive me for causing my Savior so much unspeakable torture, and teach me to be loving, patient, and kind. Jesus, let me console You. Let me ease Your suffering.

C hristianity is a triple-A religion: it is awe-inspiring, absolute, and absurd. Our all-loving and all-merciful God is awe-inspiring.

Christianity is based on moral absolutes. It is absurd to believe that in the bliss, happiness, and harmony of heaven, God would sacrifice this by humiliating and tormenting what He had created and by those He also created but did not love Him. He hung on dead wood for dead wood. Christ lost all for all. If we are all for Him, we win all for all time.

At the Palm Sunday service, the Passion of Christ was read. Many of the names of key people were mentioned, but two of the most important people were not mentioned. The names of St. John and Mary, the mother of Jesus, were left out. I was startled by this. Perhaps the two people closest to Christ were together but the farthest from the others.

Everyone wears a mask, you see, so no one can see the tears.

My heart is healing from wounds inflicted years ago.
I am content.

When I was a child, I looked in awe and amazement at the world and the thought of God. However, when I reached adulthood, the sense of awe and amazement left me. The world and God seemed more a matter of acceptance, though I still loved the Lord. Now that I am older, I look with awe and amazement at the world and God again.

When I was in college, I decided to become a Roman Catholic. I made an appointment with the priest who was assigned to my university. He arranged for me to take instructions in the church.

Every precept and every law seemed right, true, and cohesive. I readily agreed to follow them all.

I was surprised at the loud protests my parents made about my conversion. One of them threw a rosary and a crucifix at me. Nevertheless, I was conditionally baptized in the Roman Catholic Church.

After graduation, I returned home. My parents tried to keep me away from the church. My parents let me drive their car as long as I did not drive it to church.

In the winter, I walked one and a half miles to Mass when it was snowy and icy. I moved away from home because of my parents' attitude. I found a new home in the Roman Catholic Church and in the heart of Jesus, my Savior. I could never be my parents' daughter in the same obedient way. I was His daughter at that point.

So much has changed. As a child, I liked to watch fireflies on summer evenings. Now, fireflies can be compared to little soldiers for Christ. They each give a little light for a world that's growing dim. Thank you, Lord, for all Your fireflies.

I have heard Your song, Lord Jesus. It is engraved on my mind, heart, and soul forever.

I find part of the "Gloria" interesting. At the end, we say, "world without end, amen." I have said this so many times without thinking. Today, I stopped to think about what these words mean. At first, I was startled. I thought, *World without end? How can this be? Every Christian knows the world is going to end, and there will be a new heaven and a new earth.*

Then I realized that the world that does not end is God's world. Of course I believe heaven does not end, but stop and ponder what I have been saying. I just realized that God gave me the grace to look at eternity a little closer today.

Thank You, my Lord and my God. I do love You. I do not understand how some people don't love You.

My next prayer is, "Our Father, who art in heaven, give them this day the grace to know and love You."

S ometimes, our day does not go as planned. We think it is the end of the world. It isn't. The end of the world is not what we think it is. At the end of the world, Christ will come again. We will have a new heaven and earth with Him eternally.

S ometimes, I do too much, become too tired, and become
out of sorts. I regularly pray, and I work to keep my temper
in check.

In my weariness, I called upon the Lord. He came to me. "You
have given me rest, joy, contentment, and peace. You are my Rock,
my Redeemer, my joy, my light, my salvation. Though I am weak,
I am strong. Lead me on, kind light."

One reason that the rich grow richer and the poor grow poorer is that the rich are able to afford the tuition at the finest universities.

When we love God, we should go beyond the hope that a good outcome is possible. We should so firmly believe that our destiny is God and heaven that we thank Him in advance. And it won't hurt to thank Our Lady of the Angels and the saints.

In heaven, saints may enjoy varying degrees of joy. However, in God's eyes, everyone is equally one of His children.

I work hard for others. I play hard for myself. Why don't I pray hard too? I claim God is first in my life. Is He?

My husband has been attending Mass with me. I have prayed, and he has been a Catholic for thirty-nine years.

When I mentioned going to Mass one weekend, he asked, "Why should I take you to Mass? It's just a big hassle for me." I became upset. I prayed, and I pondered what I should do. Then God gave me the grace to realize two things. First, the devil loved seeing me upset. He must hate me. One son is a priest, and his sister wants to be a nun. Another son is working on his master's degree so he can help others. Still another son is married and has a daughter. All are exemplary children. That certainly warrants an attack by the devil.

God gives peace. The devil gives turmoil. Maybe Satan lost the battle with my children.

Even dearer to me is my husband. I love him so much. I so want him to know the love and joy God gives. If the devil can win my husband to his side, that would be a triumph for him and a heartbreaking loss for me.

The second thing I realized about my husband was that the more he protested becoming a Roman Catholic, the closer he came to being one.

My dear God, I thank You for loving me. I am a poor sinner. I will always love You more than anyone else because even though I'm a sinner, You have given Your life for me. Please give me the courage to give my life for You and everyone else.

I do works of mercy by doing my best to love God and others with all my mind, heart, and soul. Thank You for Your mercy.

J esus is my spiritual bridegroom. I promise to love Him forever. He is my perfect love. I will go wherever He leads me. I look at my poor love nailed to the overbearing crucifix in my hands. I look back to His Crucifixion and can clearly envision those few at Golgotha. The sky was black. All heaven raged a storm of accusation to see the King breathe His last and drop His head, bloody and cold.

I look at Christ on my crucifix. He died of suffocation when He could no longer hold His body up so He could breathe. I place my hands on either side of His arms on my crucifix to support them. I know the present year. I know I am not in Jerusalem. My act is a gesture of love. Jesus suffered thousands of years ago for the sinful acts that I do now. Perhaps a good act now helped Him then. He sees all time at once.

Jesus is my perfect love who opens the mysteries of His Father and His Brother, the Holy Spirit, who are my one love in three persons and vice versa. I await our perfect union.

I want to do what I can to love my beloved. Sometimes, I'm brave enough to suffer a redemptive love for others.

God, please allow me to know You, and consecrate myself to You as You want.

God is in charge. If it is His will, it will come about. If it is not His will, it won't.

We should always try to draw closer to God by practicing virtue. By practicing the virtue of patience, we will become more peaceful and calm, which is the opposite of the devil's strife and unrest. The hardest and most effective area to practice this is at home with our family and pets. It is easy to dismiss and walk away from people for whom we have no affection. Embodied in our relationships with the people we love is the antithesis of love—hate.

About a year and a half ago, Mother Angelica was on EWTN, the Eternal Word Television Network, promoting a coffee cup with her picture on it. I thought she was being haughty. Now, I realize I was being haughty. She truly is a saint, and she was offering a humble reminder of herself to those who might want it.

I n the sanctuaries of Roman Catholic churches during the Easter season are three different-sized candles. The smallest are used by the people in prayerful petition. The next are those of the church, which light the most holy sacrifice of the Mass. The largest is the Easter candle, which represents Christ, the Light of the World.

Our Lord, Jesus Christ, gave Himself beyond any understanding humankind can visualize or grasp. We must be willing to wager everything. Gradually, we may become the warm wax on which God may place His stamp.

Sister Mary Faith

I find peace and joy in knowing that all we have to do is raise our eyes to see God, the Blessed Virgin, and all the saints in heaven.

Then of course, we may look down and close our eyes in prayer.

I would like to see an optional form of our morning offering. Now, we go to Mary through Jesus by saying, "Oh, Jesus, through the immaculate heart of Mary, through Your sacred heart …" We put Mary first and then Jesus. In an optional form, we would reverse the order: "Oh, Jesus, through Your sacred heart and through the immaculate heart of Mary …"

Sister Mary Faith

Love's Fire

I gazed upward.
I did not know what to expect.
I saw soft, brown eyes
And a careful, gentle gaze.

I knew I was not the first.
That made me a little sad.
I felt fear and wonder.
Will others follow me?
There was guilt and gladness.

I savored your tenderness.
Your touch was measured.
It was so light and slow.
Your hand cupped my breast.
Suddenly, I felt flushed.

I wanted to drink heavily.
The wine was all of you.
All of you lay upon me.
Is this how it is done?
Is this how we are made one?

Sister Mary Faith

You moved rapidly with rhythm.
As you thrust in and out.
I moaned and groaned.
Every nerve was on fire.
I managed to speak.
I gasped, "More, more, more."

I felt a joyous crescendo.
Your tightened biceps relaxed.
You smiled and questioned.
"Was it good for you?"
"Yes," I emphasized.
We gently held each other.
What sweet peace we knew.
We were no longer two.
He and she are now we.

I started to walk in a forest. The verdant leaves forming a canopy over the area darkened it. I saw water with a sandy beach. I had grown tired of walking and decided to swim in the water to refresh myself. The sand was quicksand. I began to sink. I prayed to the Holy Trinity to save me from death.

Quickly, I was on firm ground. The forest changed. It was no longer quiet and dark. Now it was light, and birds of every kind sang melodiously. My soul's burden of sin and darkness was lifted. I sang praises to God, my Savior.

Sister Mary Faith

Sister Mary Faith

The key to life is love, and the key to love is life.

The sanctuary of my church has been remodeled. It is now simple and has a beautiful stone floor with Jerusalem crosses in three places.

The floor has an element of being permanent. The crucifix has been replaced. The new one is surrounded by light. It is perfect. Christ is the Light of the World. Light comes from His Crucifixion. The sanctuary is more like God, our Trinity.

Is simple and permanent.

In my weariness, I called upon You, Lord. You gave me rest, joy, contentment, and peace. You are my Rock, my Redeemer, my joy, light, and salvation.

To take care of the soul, it is necessary to take care of the body.

P eople can be angry with people they don't know. That is why the term *road rage* was invented. One driver gets in the way of another. One driver becomes enraged because his sense of direction is at stake. This is rare. Normally, people become enraged when loved ones threaten their sense of self-direction.

It's much easier to ignore strangers than those who are often in our pathway or near us.

We accommodate handicapped workers so they can work. Shouldn't we accommodate volunteer workers even more for the services they provide from the heart and soul that they are not paid for?

I t can be a challenge to tell the difference between righteous indignation and sinful anger. God is the same today, forever, and always. He is good, merciful, peaceful, and loving.

To teach the human race, He may chastise either them or Himself. The Jewish nation endured the flood and was saved by and for those on Noah's ark. God did not spare the rod during the Babylonian exile of His favored nation.

Even today, Jewish people celebrate Passover.

Jesus whipped the money changers.

God is not fickle. His nature is constant. We should be constant in righteous acts rather than sinful anger. We can do this by constantly striving to be like our God by being good, merciful, peaceful, and loving.

Sometimes, I feel frustrated. I do not have time to do all the daily duties for God that I have to do.

You are the pitcher in this eternal game of life. It is my job to hit Your ball out of the park and score the team. The pitcher is given all the glory. It is both right and just.

The truest love is silent love that goes unnoticed and gently leads others to do the work of our Savior.

A multitude of factors challenge our minds, hearts, bodies, and souls. One day, for instance, my husband is concerned and generous with his immediate family, while another day, he is concerned with the welfare of his community family.

My cross is loving other people who I feel are unlovable. My Lord's cross is loving me and forgiving me for finding others unlovable.

I became overly tired. My husband didn't keep promises he made to do things. My puppy, Angel (often a misnomer), barked very loud and often. She pooped inside and crunched my SD card with my photos on it. I totally lost it. I became unhinged; I screamed and took God's name in vain. I also banged dishes and said a couple of four-letter words. One of the dishes broke.

I cried and resolved to go to confession the next day. The next morning, I fixed breakfast for my husband and puppy. I had asked for forgiveness from them the night before. In the confessional, I told the priest I'd been pondering the necessity of commending my spirit to God.

Interestingly enough, the readings at Mass were about St. Peter, and they started off well—walking on the water and then slipping only to have the Lord save him. The reading fit my situation perfectly. I started off well but then ventured out too far, let my emotional winds take control, and found myself sinking. But by the grace of God, I am raised to grace once more.

My husband bought me a fine diamond ring from an even finer jeweler, a very well-known authority on jewels. I took my diamond ring to have the jeweler reappraise it. I felt confident that the ring's value had increased. I was shocked when my jeweler told me that I had a small chip on the stone, which rendered it valueless.

I know an even finer jeweler than the first, and he is also a lapidary. He can take a gem with a small chip and recut and reshape the jewel until it is priceless. I am sure you have heard of this jeweler and lapidary. His name is God.

A neighbor severed our thirty-year friendship when I asked her for a ride to church and asked about her health. She would not accept my hand at church for the sign of peace, nor would she accept my phone calls afterward.

On December 18, 2016, I read in our church bulletin that her husband was in need of prayers. I called their home. When he answered, I asked about his health. He explained about his malady and recent serious surgery. I told him how worried I was about him and expressed relief that he was well. Then I asked him if he knew who was calling, and he answered, "Yes, Mary, I do." His tone was warm and friendly. I bridged another gap over troubled waters.

A very dear friend of more than thirty years and I shared dinner one night at a fine restaurant. She devotes her life to helping others. She was one of the four people who started Birthright. Throughout the meal, we talked about the graces God had given us to help His people. We were and are both grateful for His abounding benevolence. We gave thanks for all these blessings. I came home and realized that we had forgotten to give Him thanks for the food He had given us.

A beautiful Jewish family sat at the next table. They probably remembered to thank God for their meal. It was a humbling experience.

My poor God! What have I done to You?

Forgive me for I know not what I am doing. Truly You are the Son of God!

T o exercise my spiritual muscles, I try to practice virtue in some way.

One virtue I should practice more is to enter the confessional and ask my Savior's forgiveness.

As I enter the confessional, I confess the same sins to the same priest. I feel that I should record my confession. Only You, O Lord, can redeem this situation. I give it entirely to You.

The most important words in the New Testament are, "Let it be done unto me according to Thy will."

We agree, and pray, "Thy will be done." We should ardently desire that our Father's will be done.

My soul has known very light and very dark times. During the light times, God's vision shines brightly. During the dark times, His vision does not shine at all. I try not to question His existence.

Presently, I have been enjoying a time of light. I know only too well, however, that a dark fog will envelop my soul again. Still, I hope for a bright end. Everyone in heaven has known both light and dark times. Everyone there has known something of death and life.

I try to love God, help others, and earn money in my career. Unfortunately, the importance I place on these actions is not always in that order.

I enjoy online games. In school, I was taught to be very competitive. Now, I believe it's better to enjoy the game no matter the outcome.

I can spend four hours a day playing an online game. It is unusual, but it happens. I find it hard to spend one or two minutes in prayer. When I meditate, I close my mind and open my heart to God.

When playing games of chance, you will mislead yourself if you plan on being a winner too often, but if you take a chance on God, you will always win.

M y relationship with my husband has changed. He was afraid that I'd leave him with no money. He wanted to put me in a mental hospital so I would not be able to spend the money.

Predator

I was looking for my husband-to-be. He should have every golden, not sterling, quality.

We started dating. I fell in love. He was good, kind, and gentle. We laughed and talked for hours. I missed him so much when he left for home.

I remember his grin before I walked down the aisle.

He could not have children.

I wanted many, but I loved him more.

We lived in wedded bliss for years.

He and I fought occasionally.

As we aged, we were less dependent on wealth.

We were more dependent on health.

He is slowly dying. He is frightened.

The chemo has clouded his thoughts.

I am no longer a bride. I am a beast.

Like all beasts, I must be put in a pen.

He is no longer my groom.
He is the broom to sweep me away.
Now he is predatory.
I love him still, not so much the money in the will.

I watched Mass on the television again today. I was impressed by the face of an elderly acolyte. He was listening to the readings. His face looked like that of a child who had heard something new. He had. He had heard the good news.

I can tell that I am aging. I have a sense of happiness when my prescriptions are refilled when I need them.

Tonight, a dear friend told me to take my arms and put my weight on her so I wouldn't fall. As I wearily stepped off the curb and onto my walker, I was afraid that I'd hurt her if we fell together. Thankfully, all went well, and we made it just fine to the sidewalk.

G od is all-good, all-loving, and all-merciful. The repentant sinner may enter heaven. He created people for joy and happiness. Each person must make a conscious decision to follow God to enter bliss.

We all know suffering. Our minds, bodies, and souls are one. If one part suffers, the rest are affected. When time stops and only pain exists, suffering can be at its worst.

O f all my sufferings I endure when I am ill, the greatest is not being able to attend Mass.

The thought of death should not alarm Christians. When Christians die, they simply move their address upward.

At death, the heart stops beating. If we have been faithful, the heart of the soul will continue beating forever.

Sister Mary Faith

When my husband and I were dating, the movie *You Light Up My Life* and the song by the same title were released. This song became our special love song. It is also my song of love for the Lord.

For He lights up my life.

Live a life of service to others regardless of the cost.

Mary accepted His death.

Jesus Christ ascends to heaven.

The agony in the garden.

"I Am."
Jesus was afraid but resolute.

All things will work toward the good for those who love God.

Printed in the United States
By Bookmasters